The Borrowed Breath

Poems of Touching God

By Don MacLeod

Bound & Determined
Minneapolis

The Borrowed Breath

Copyright © 2014-2017 Don MacLeod

All rights reserved under the Berne Convention

No part of this publication may be reproduced, distributed, or transmitted in any form or by any means, including photocopying, recording, or other electronic or mechanical methods, without the prior written permission of the publisher, except in the case of brief quotations embodied in critical reviews and certain other noncommercial uses permitted by copyright law.

For permission requests, write to the publisher at:
"Attention: Permissions Coordinator"
Bound & Determined
2637 27th Ave. S.
Suite 219
Minneapolis, MN 55406

Or email bound.determined@gmail.com

First Bound & Determined Edition

ISBN 978-1-947261-01-3
Revised

Dedication

To my wonderful teacher Prem Rawat for showing me my true self, for teaching me peace and love.

Table of Contents

The Darkness Rose

The Blind

Because Ellen Can't

I Do Not Look Immortal

The Impatience of the Emotions

I Will Always Love You

The Unliving

Open Your Heart

Surrender

There Are Those Days

Wave

River of Life

There Is This Dark Side

You Want To Dance With God?

Imagination Running Wild

The Hidden

Jeanne

The Darkness Roams

I Was There

The God We Pray To

Boat
Next
My Heart
Taste of Infinity
The World Is a Lonely Place
Fire Within
You Were Always There
When Was the Last Time
Birthday Wish for Krista
Where Is the Rain
What If I Told You
If I Told You My Heart
And That Is How My Heart Gets Full
Driftwood
Julie's Wish
Letter
Remember
Where Has the Wind Gone
Where Were You When My Heart Did Open
The Door to Infinity
The Borrowed Breath
Acknowledgements

The Darkness Rose

The Darkness rose
It said, "I am powerful"
I said, "Yes"
It said, "I am more powerful than you"
I said, "Yes"
It said, "I can envelope you in despair"
I said, "Yes"
It said, "I can envelope cities in despair"
I said, "You can"
It said, "I can swallow and envelope entire countries in darkness and despair"
I said, "Yes, you can"
It said, "I can take this world and enclose it in hate and anger"
I said, "Yes, yes you can"
It said, "I will take you first"
I lit a candle

The Blind

I Walk Through This World blindly
Occasionally I see the other blind that I walk with
Occasionally they see me
We are looking straight ahead or at our seeing devices
But our seeing devices are blind as well
We think we are seeing
But our eyes aren't even open
Our hearts are too afraid to see
Fear is our constant companion
Grooming us for this world that we cannot see
Reminding us how to be for the things that we cannot see
Coaching us in a world that doesn't exist
Pretending to protect our hearts when it knows it can't
Our hearts get hurt no matter what we do to protect them
So I say
What's the difference
Why try to protect something that's going to get hurt any
Live out loud
Show your heart
Love people with all your heart
Don't care if they're going to love you back

You're going to love them anyway
So why fake it
Why pretend like you don't
Love them out loud
It's the only way to not be blind
You start to cure your own blindness
Others will see
They will want to cure their own blindness

Because Ellen Can't

Because Ellen can no longer paint with her hands and fingers
Can I paint the paintings that she left, but with words
She left so many paintings unpainted
I can feel them
We talked of them
Some
The others just hung around her like ghosts
I could almost touch them
Can you put a painting in words instead
Can you take colors that you can almost taste and make them seen
I know you can describe an image, but can you really paint it with words
Should you try
Should I try
Will someone catch them as they fly through the ethers
Can they do them the justice they need done them
Will they fly on the pages as they do through the air
Can they
Ellen made so many fly
She touched the sky when she painted
She flew

She touched the depths of her being and put them on canvas and paper
She took magic and made it visible to the human eye
She took shadows and made them light
Her real and only desire was to be of God and to express that
That's what crazy people do and boy was she crazy
Totally insane with the desire to express her Creator
Express the depths of what she felt
And she FELT DEEPLY

I Do Not Look Immortal

I do not look immortal
I am an aging man to this world
But that is how I look
I will shed this skin and move on
But I will not die
I will come into a new skin and be young
Because I am immortal

The Impatience of the Emotions

The impatience of the emotions is overwhelming sometimes. They push, they shove, they scream and cry and yet we want them to stay in their little box and be quiet. I have been in several meetings where a person said "There is no room for emotions here." I wanted to say that we would have to clear the room if that were true, but I didn't.

I Will Always Love You

Here I sit falling in love with you.
I will never tell you like so many gutless men before me.
I will fall in love and never speak of it.
That love sits quietly repressed in the heart.
Unspoken, unrequited, untouchable.
I will never tell you, for so many reasons.
You have a lover.
You are younger.
You are too beautiful.
I have seen death.
I have lived with death.
I am immortal because of it.
You are a delicate flower that should not be crushed.
I would crush you with my sadness.
I would crush you with my fear.
I would crush you with my want.
I will not tell you.
I will watch you grow.
I will watch you flourish.
I will watch you find another love.
I will watch you live your life.
I will watch you find the shortness of your life.
I will watch you find death.
I am immortal.

I will watch you be reborn and I will fall in love with you again.

The Unliving

We are the unliving
Unliving our lives
Not wanting the life we live
Doing nothing to change it
Doing nothing to break the cycle
Dragging ourselves through the day
Afraid to ask for help
Afraid to tell the truth
Fear is our constant companion
Small most days, but constant
It dictates our every word
It dictates our every decision
This small worm, an infection making us the unliving
We have to take the medicine to cure this infection
We have to take the medicine that will make us brave
That medicine is called love
It's a powerful medicine
But it's hard for us to swallow
We don't think that we deserve it
We fear it's not true
We fear
Take your medicine
Share your medicine
Receive the medicine you are given

There is an abundant supply in every breath
Encourage others to take their medicine
We can not live this life in fear
This world can not live this life in fear
Love is not sex
Sex is not love
We get those confused
Love comes from the heart
Love is received by the heart
It's time to stop this unliving
It's time just stop this unloving
For all of us
It's time for all of us to live our lives
It's time for all of us to love our lives

Open Your Heart

Open your heart. Find me. I am there, your hidden lover. Waiting with each breath for you to know I love you. To feel my love, my passion, my Desire for you. I wait and will wait until that moment you claim me as yours. Take me in your arms, embrace me. Know that we are one, that there is no separation. That all you want is me, all I want is you. Make me yours. I will make you mine.

Embrace me.

Surrender

Ultimately we will all surrender completely to the will of God.
We could live our entire life under the will of God.
Why wait until the last few seconds?

There Are Those Days

There are the days when the pain comes on unbidden
The pain is always there, but there are "those" days
The pain comes unbidden
With no warning
It sits
It waits
It waits
It watches
It does nothing more than being there
That is a lot on those days
"Those" days
The ones "we" don't speak about
The ones "we" hide from
Hide from everyone and try to hide from ourselves
But, we can't hide it from ourselves very long
Because it sits there
And waits
And watches
And is there

Wave

There is a wave that comes and calls to be ridden
It gently laps at first
Then it slowly grows stronger with its magnetic pull
Whispering, knowing you want to ride it
It pulls and tugs slowly at you
You have ridden this wave before
You know the immense feelings that it brings
You know you should resist
You know the pain it brings
Yet it so attractive
It touches one part of you so gently

River of Life

I was sitting by the River of Life and saw my reflection.
Not the reflection you see, I see, but the reflection God sees.

There Is This Dark Side

There is this dark side that rests in you
There is this dark side that rests in me
There is this dark side that doesn't rest
There is this dark side that creates havoc
Sometimes big, sometimes small
There is this dark side that does not want to be seen
There is this dark side that hides from full light
There is this dark side that wants you to fear
There is this dark side that wants you to hide
There IS this dark side
There is this light side that rests in you
There is this light side that rests in me
There is this light side that rests
There is this light side that creates peace
Sometimes big, sometimes small
There is this light side that wants to be seen
There is this light side that casts away the illusion of darkness
There is this light side that wants you to feel safe
There is this light side that wants you to shine
There IS this light side

You Want To Dance With God?

You want to dance with God
Stand in your heart
Wait with open arms
Listen for the Divine Silence
Move to that rhythm
God will come

Some say that dancing with God is dangerous
It IS
You will completely Lose Yourself

The Divine will come

There the music is played you will dance to
There you will hear the rhythm to move to

Imagination Running Wild

I could see her running through the field. Bouncing up and down and spinning like a little child. Well, she was a little child and she should be bouncing like one. Ah to be 7 years old running through a field smelling flower after flower. Feeling one tall sprig of grass after another, imagination running wild.

I was clear she was not seeing what I was seeing. Was she by a castle? Was she dancing with unicorns, or was she just seeing herself all grown up without a care in the world? It didn't matter. The joy on her face was beautiful whatever she was seeing.

The Hidden

I can feel it.
Hovering there.
Waiting.
What is it?
What is it that lies there below the surface?
Is it dangerous?
Surely it's dangerous if it is hiding?
Maybe not.
The gentle creatures hide too.
They don't want to be preyed upon.
Which is this thing lying in wait?
Predator or prey.
Do I investigate, or assume that is predator and not prey.
Why is it something so hidden can draw me so much?
Pulling me in asking me to caress it.
Surely it's prey and not predator?
Either way it's not safe, but I must know.
Whatever you are, step forward.
Ah. There it is. I still don't know which you are?
The sadness is there, but I never know which one you are.
Will you pull me in to an abyss, or will you lift me up after I have caressed and soothed the wound that you are presenting?

Jeanne

I love the gentleness of my friend
I love the anger of my friend
I love the power she holds
I love the power she releases
I love the torment she feels at the wrongs in the world
I love the attempts she makes to right them
I love the willingness she has to fall on her face
I love the willingness she has to get up again if it kills her
I love the amount of strength it takes her to get up every day
I love the times she is weak and can't move
I love the passion she shares with the world
I love the big feelings she doesn't know what to do with
I love the struggle she has to not be her
I love the struggle she has to be her
I love the way she fights to stay alive
I love the fight she fights to be
I love the person she is
I love the person she was
I love the person she is going to be

The Darkness Roams

The darkness roams the halls of our minds and beings
Poking here, pushing there, instilling fear where it can
Pushing doubt to the front of our awareness
The darkness calls, it beckons us with lavish lies of comfort and joy
Then pulls us in with dark remembrances that it feeds us over and over again
Let me comfort you it says
Telling the lies of our failures
Telling the lies of our faults
Telling the lies of our unforgivable things
Feel the joy of the suffering that you do so well
Insinuating itself into our everything, blinding our true vision
Reminding us of every little thing done or said wrong
Calling us deeper into our deserved suffering
Laying waste to any hope that we or our actions are redeemable
Opening the pit within showing us where we belong
Calling us deeper and deeper
The darkness grows, reaching out to our every fault
Our suffering is so great and deserved

Play with me, it says
I know you better, it says
I look after you, it says
I show you the truth, it says

But the redeemer walks those paths too
Handing out forgiveness we don't know how to accept
We have practiced the suffering so long
Handing out the compassion we don't know how to accept
We have practiced discordance so long
Beckoning to us with gifts of love we don't know how to accept
We are practiced at darkness, we don't know ways of light
The redeemer walks within, shining light so the shadows flee
We are practiced at darkness and think we are losing parts of ourselves
The redeemer drops acceptance on our hurt places
We are practiced at darkness and think the hurt is precious
The redeemer walks with gentle steps of love
We are practiced at darkness and think it odd that our pain can dissipate

The redeemer beacons us with real comfort and joy
The darkness tells us it's a lie
The redeemer shines brightly and says, follow my way
The darkness tells us we will lose what is ours
The redeemer shines brighter and shows the way
The redeemer brings light to the darkness and we lose ourselves
The redeemer brings light to the darkness and we find ourselves
The redeemer brings light to the darkness and We become the light

I Was There

I was there at the beginning
I was there when the first breath was taken
I was there when love began
I was there when you were created
I was there when you had your first thought
I was there at your first step
I am there as you aged
I am there as you approach death
I am there at your death
I am there after your death
Why oh why are you afraid

The God We Pray To

The God we pray to is the God of our pagan forefathers.
The God we pray to is the God of myths.
We do not pray to the true God.
We pray to the God of our ideas, of our religions
We pray to the God that we believe is like Santa Claus granting our wishes
We pray to a God in heaven so far away
We say that God is omnipresent, but we don't really believe it
God is in heaven so far away
This is the God of our pagan forefathers
The true God is not so far away
Our true God is close
God being omnipresent, is then within every atom of our being
Not far away in Heaven
Why have we forsaken God and put him so far away
When our God is ever present, in every breath, in every day, in every moment
When we pray, it's assuming a separation
As if God doesn't know our every want, our every desire, our every need
We pray because we feel lost
We pray with hope that we are not alone

We pray that there is a connection to God
Then what should we pray
We pray that we see
We pray that we see God close
We pray that we see God so close that God is all we see
We pray that we see the world through God's eyes
We pray that we see God not so far away

That we look at the world with compassion
That we look at the world with Grace
That we look at the world with love
That we look at the world through God's eyes

Boat

In our heart lies a boat.
The boat is there to convey us through our lives.
We believe that we have to swim the whole way, but it is not true.
Climb in the boat. Let it take you gently, effortlessly to the destinations in your life.

Next

Next
Next
Next
Each breath
Coming
Going
One at a time
Like drops of rain
Falling on my heart
God saying he loves me

My Heart

My heart
Your heart
Is there a difference
No my beloved
There is none
They beat together as one
The sound of each breath
Coming and going
Syncs the beating
My heart
Your heart
There is no difference

Taste of Infinity

I tasted Infinity last night
Right on the tip of my tongue
Its sweetness was overwhelming
We danced in the moonlight of many earths
The suns were pinpricks, too many to count
The silence was deafening, but was a beautiful song
Our hearts were joy and we became one

The World Is a Lonely Place

The world is a lonely place without friends, or is it. I was lucky early on to realize that loneliness is a call to God. The call does not go unanswered. It is our song, our hearts saying I need to feel you, I need to know you are there. We need to learn to hear the response. We need to learn to hear and feel the answer. That filling up that makes you explode. But sometimes, it's hard to let go of the loneliness and longing. That emptiness in our hearts that calls to the creator. That emptiness is a gift that we do not want to give away.

Our heart is like a cup. It fills, it empties, it fills, it empties.

Fire Within

So much of us needs warmth
So much of us needs comfort
So much of us needs light
There is a beautiful fire in each of our hearts
It gives us warmth
It gives us comfort
It gives us light
It gives us love

You Were Always There

People look at you and in their mind, you are the one that lost her.
Seeing you reminds them she is not there.
They have lost her too, but she was yours.
They were hers.
They have a hole in them that they don't know how to fill.
They got to spend time with her, because you were there.
You were always there with her.
They got to know a deeper part of her, because you were there.
They got to see her unfold her wings getting ready to fly, because you were there to catch her if she fell.
You were always there.
She was a friend, their friend, but you were always there with her.
Yes you were.
As she said, "You make the world safe for me."
That's why you were always there.
When you weren't with her, she knew you were still making the world safe for her.
That's why you were always there.
They don't know the things you know.
They don't know the suffering being in this world brought to her.

You did.
That's why you were always there.
When the world said, "You have six months to live," you faltered and she felt you weren't there.
You weren't there as you had fallen.
Your wings had been bent and you could not support even yourself.
You were not able to catch her as the weight was so heavy.
When you finally got up off the ground, she was not there.
You wanted to be there.
When she came back, you tried to always be there.
It wasn't the same.
You knew she was going to fall and no one could catch her.
No matter how hard they tried or how strong they were, they could not catch her, you could not catch her.
When she finally fell the last time after so much…, so much what?
So much suffering?
Yes, but so much joy at living longer.
2 1/2 years past her expiration date.
But then she fell for good that one last time.

Gone from this world and the friends looked on.
They fell with her, holes in their hearts.
Her friends looked on as you fell and fell and fell and fell.
They didn't have the wings to fly.
They knew you had lost half your soul.
Not just a hole in your heart like theirs.
Even if they could help, you couldn't reach out to grab hold.
Time has passed and now you see her friends every so often.
You are too big of a reminder that she's not here anymore.
So they avoid you, but not consciously.
They almost whisper when they talk to you so they don't disturb your grief.
If they did, it would disturb their own.
They know you lost more and don't feel they deserve to grieve.
You want them to, because they do deserve to.
You want them to share their memories of her.
That helps fill our holes, that empty spot in our hearts where she lived.
When she was here, you felt safe.
That's why she was always there.
Now that she is gone, the world is not so safe.

She is no longer there.
Friends promise to stay in touch.
They can't, they don't know how and you don't know how.
She is not there.
Her friends liked her a lot more than you and liked you because you were with her.
But that's OK.
You liked her a lot more also and not them as much too.
You understand.
An angel, a divine being left the planet.
She is no longer there.
The hole is there and will always be.
For them and for you, because she is not there.
I am not there.

Birthday Wish for Krista

That when you judge yourself, you feel the love of those that love you.
That when your imperfections are bigger than a house, you know you are loved anyway.
That you can see what you are good at and accept it.
That you see that you are a good person no matter what you think, or how awful you think something you have done is.
That you see what you are not very good at and easily accept it. If you can change it, you will.
That you are able to love yourself as much as you love others. You are your best friend, don't say bad things about you EVER, EVER, EVER.
When you look in the mirror, you see what the people that love you see.
When I look at you, I see beauty.
When I look at you, I see your sadness.
When I look at you, I see light.
When I look at you, I see the hurt you think will never go away.
When I look at you, I see love.
When I look at you, I see kindness.
When I look at you, I see your heart very close to the surface.

When I look at you, I see your pain that kindness will cure.
When I look at you, I see intelligence.
When I look at you, I see willingness.
When I look at you, I see an infinite joy waiting to come forth.
Walk in the light
Be in the light
Stay in the light
You are the light

When Was the Last Time

When was the last time you saw what was around you?
When was the last time you stopped and looked?
It's so easy to walk from the house to the car knowing everything that is there on the way.
You've seen it all before, but did you see it?
Did you hear the birds sing this morning, or were they quiet?
The trees noticed you as you passed by. Did you notice them?
What did you notice?
Anything?
Or are you just blindly walking through the world already having seen it?

Where Is the Rain

Where is the rain that falls so quietly
The rain that washes everything,
EVERYTHING away
The rain that waters my parched heart
The rain that fills me
The rain that soothes my mind
The rain that soothes my selfishness

It is here
It is NOW

The rain that fills my every desire
The rain falls on me every day, every hour,
every moment
It is every breath

What If I Told You

What if I told you I spoke with the Gods
What if I told you that we were friends
What if I told you that I see them dancing in the stars
Would you believe me
Would I seem insane
Maybe I am
But I do see them
And We Dance
And we sing
I don't know why I get to dance with them
I don't know why they chose me
But oh is it ever fun

If I Told You My Heart

If I told you my heart
Would you listen
Would you be kind
Could you take it in
Could you be gentle
If I told you my heart
Would it be safe
Would it be safe
Could it be safe
Could it be safe
If I told you my heart
What would you do
What would your heart do
Could your heart take in
Could your heart be open
If I told you my heart
Would you hear my pain
Would you hear my fear
Could you sooth my pain
Could you sooth my fear
If I told you my heart
Could I trust you
Could I know that your love is true
Would I know your heart
Would you let me know yours
If you told me your heart
Would I listen
Would I be kind

And That Is How My Heart Gets Full

Written from the bottom up

I am out in this world and I am part of this world
Things happen that are not so fun sometimes
Something happens and it triggers a lot of feelings
A confrontation, a sad word, an old memory, a sense of loss
The world, the mind, the thoughts, the anxiety, the fears, the problems, they all swirl around in my head and this is not what I want
My heart's desire is to be at peace, not to have this tornado running through me
I know how to stop and find calm
Making the conscious decision to open up and to allow the peace to make its presence known
Knowing that the peace, the calm I am looking for is within
Being physically still and closing my eyes
Watching the light approach
Breathing slowly
The mind calms
The heart opens gently and slowly
And that is how my heart gets full

Driftwood

We just stood there quietly watching the river flow by. Beautiful driftwood slowly moved by us. It was almost as if it was saying "Hi. Slow down. What's your hurry?"
What was our hurry?
Was there really an urgency?
Couldn't we just stay here and watch the water go by?

Julie's Wish

My wish for you
That you know what you see is NOT how things really look
That you see everything you think doesn't really matter, because you can think anything
That you see it is a gift to be who you are
That you see that you are a beautiful soul
That you see your big heart
That you see you are loved for who you are, right now, not for who you think you are or should be
That you see what God sees when She looks at you

Letter

Let her be
Let her love
Let her enjoy
Let her be free
Let her fly
Let her find herself
Let her sing
Let her cry
Let her be silent
Let her be alone
Let her go

Remember

Remember
We stood there
In the beauty
In the light
In the love
Waiting in anticipation
Waiting in acceptance
Waiting in peace
Wanting nothing
Wanting everything
Wanting love
Knowing nothing
Knowing everything
Knowing love
Feeling joy
Feeling beauty
Feeling whole
Remember

Where Has the Wind Gone

Where has the wind gone?
The one that opens our wings and allows us to fly.
The one that lifts our spirits up above our mundane thoughts.
The one that takes us in its arms and comforts us.
The one that tells us every moment we are alive is a blessing, regardless.
The one that gives us the courage to do the things we must.
The one that allows us to see we are all equal, that no one is above another.
The one that cracks our hearts open and makes us love and be loved more.
The one that tells us we are loved in every moment.
I will tell you where that wind is.
It is in every breath as it goes in and out.
It spreads our wings to fly.
It lifts our spirits above everything.
It gives us deep comfort.
It is a blessing in every moment.
It is courage.
It is equal in everyone good or bad.
It opens our hearts.
It is Love.

Where Were You When My Heart Did Open

Where were you when my heart did open
Where were you when it began to sing
The spark of life shown brightly
As it hung amongst the stars
The breath that came was not truly mine
But borrowed from where you are
I can only find contentment when I see you in my feigned sleep
That is where I hang out with the Gods of old
We dance and chat and sometimes sing real slow
All they want to do is play
But my heart, my heart, is looking for the one

The Door to Infinity

The door to Infinity opened this morning
It opened down not sideways like a normal door, which was curious
Light spilled from it gently, beckoning
Whispering in words only my heart could understand
The world around the door became more alive, but the light called
Not like a Siren's call, but like a mother soothing a baby's cry
I knew this is what I had always wanted
I knew this is what everyone wanted
I was being given a gift, a chance, an opportunity
Thoughts, doubts, fears were nowhere to be seen
I could gaze at this doorway forever or I could go in
There was no question, even though I knew I would lose myself completely
There would be no more I
I went to the doorway and was taken in

The Borrowed Breath

Think of the most precious thing you own
Think
Now if you took your breath away, how precious is it
Now tell me what is your most precious thing
Yes, your breath and it's not even yours
You have to give every one back, as they each are borrowed
So your most precious thing is not even yours
How does that feel
We have no grasp of the thing most dear to us
We have virtually no control of its coming and going
We are helpless to that thing that powers each breath
Some day it will take the last one from us
No more borrowing
And how many were we grateful for
How many did we see as the most precious thing
So many we took without notice, without gratitude
Like they didn't really matter
Each and every one, a divine gift, unnoticed and insignificant
But really our most precious thing of all

Acknowledgements

Thank you:

Chandler Bolt for inspiring me to believe I could publish a book and giving me the tools to do it.

Tom Corson-Knowles for your YouTube videos on how to format and publish a book.

Hal Elrod for "The Miracle Morning". You helped me change my thinking patterns in a wonderful way.

Monica Matos for helping me select these poems and editing.

David MacLeod for editing and giving brotherly love and support when I needed it.

My favorite sister Deb MacLeod for editing and giving sisterly love, support and riding in a sled backwards.

Midtown Writers Group for all your support and love and being such awesome writers. You inspire me every week.

Lorenzo at A la Salsa restaurant for allowing your space to be used for 10 years to write then read every Saturday. Selena and the rest of the staff as well for looking after us during that time.

Jeanne Bain for inspiring me to write, loving me, getting me, being your weird self, loving your people, miraculously getting well, staying on the planet and just being awesome.

Joe MacLeod, my father, for being a poet and somehow passing that on without ever sharing your poetry with me. Tag, you're it.

Mary Virginia Swicord MacLeod, my mom, for being my biggest fan. For telling me stories as a child. For being your wonderful self. For seeing and knowing me.

Ellen Finholt MacLeod you lovely being. I am amazed at what you have become. Angelic does not describe it. Being your secretary taught me to write. Sharing your struggle to live made me a writer. I miss you being on the planet, but look at what you made me do.

Last things

If you liked this book, please leave me feedback

https://www.amazon.com/dp/1947261010

Thank you for reading

I don't know exactly how to say this, but it is what I try to convey in my poetry. You know those moments, the ones that you wish you could sustain. Like the way you feel when you see a beautiful sunset or sunrise. The moment you see a wild animal being free and you feel that freedom, that connection they have. Or being by the ocean, a river or stream and a peacefulness engulfs you. The beauty is almost overwhelming in those moments. Those are the moments we feel the connection to our deepest self and to that thing that sustains us. This is what my teacher Prem Rawat taught me how to find and connect to every day many years ago. He showed me the way to focus inside and touch that place whenever and wherever I want.

As I have gotten older and learned to sustain it, it really has become available all the time if I choose and remember. I have learned to focus on something other than my thoughts and connect to something more beautiful than I could have imagined. So I thought I would invite you to check it out for yourselves. Peace, tranquility and joy are so possible.

www.timelesstoday.com
www.theypi.net
www.wopg.org

www.ingramcontent.com/pod-product-compliance
Lightning Source LLC
Chambersburg PA
CBHW071756080526
44588CB00013B/2267